Painting and drawing

wax crayons

M. Àngels Comella

Silver Burdett Press, Parsippany, New Jersey

For Carla who always asks
"How do you do this?"

Painting and drawing
Other books in this series:

Poster paints
Watercolors

"Wax Crayons" (Ceras)
First published 1995 in Spanish by Parramón Ediciones S.A.
Gran Via de les Corts Catalanes, 322-324
08004 Barcelona, Spain

Text: M. Ángels .Comella
Illustrations: M. Ángels Comella
English Translation: Jonathan Bennett

First published in 1998 in the United States by

Silver Burdett Press
A Division of Simon & Schuster
299 Jefferson Road, Parsippany, NJ 07054

Library of Congress Cataloging-in-Publication Data
Comella, M. Àngels.
Creyones/por M. Àngels Comella.
p. cm.
Originally published: Barcelona, Spain: Parramón, 1995.
Includes index.
Summary: Explains how to create unusual effects and textures using wax crayons.
1. Crayon drawing—Technique—Juvenile literature. 2. Crayons—Juvenile literature. 3 Color drawing—Technique—Juvenile literature. [1. Crayon drawing—Technique. 2. Drawing—Technique. 3. Spanish language materials.] I. Title. II. Series: Comella, M. Àngels. Painting and drawing.

ND870.C66313 1997 96-32334
741.2'3—dc20. CIP AC

ISBN 0-382-39851-3 (LSB) 1 2 3 4 5 6 7 8 9 10
ISBN 0-382-39848-3 (pbk) 1 2 3 4 5 6 7 8 9 10

Printed and bound in Spain.

When you want to make a picture, do you think about which materials you will use to create the effects you want? You might choose different types of paper, crayons, pens, inks, or paints.

This book will show you how to created unusual effects and textures using wax crayons. Each technique is explained with step-by-step instructions. *At the back of the book, there is more information about materials and where to find them.*

When you have practiced the techniques shown here, you might try out your own ideas and invent new techniques.

This book won't tell you what to draw. You'll have to decide that for yourself. Many artists find inspiration for their work from people they have seen, places they have visited, stories they have heard, or even dreams they have had. They look at objects and patterns around them to get ideas. Many artists keep a sketch book of ideas.

When you have an idea for a picture, you might want to write it down or make a quick sketch. Then you need to develop your idea. The pictures and techniques in this book could help you to create effects you hadn't thought of before.

When you see this symbol in the book, you must ask an adult to help you. **!**

A BOX OF WAX CRAYONS

Wax crayons can give all kinds of effects.

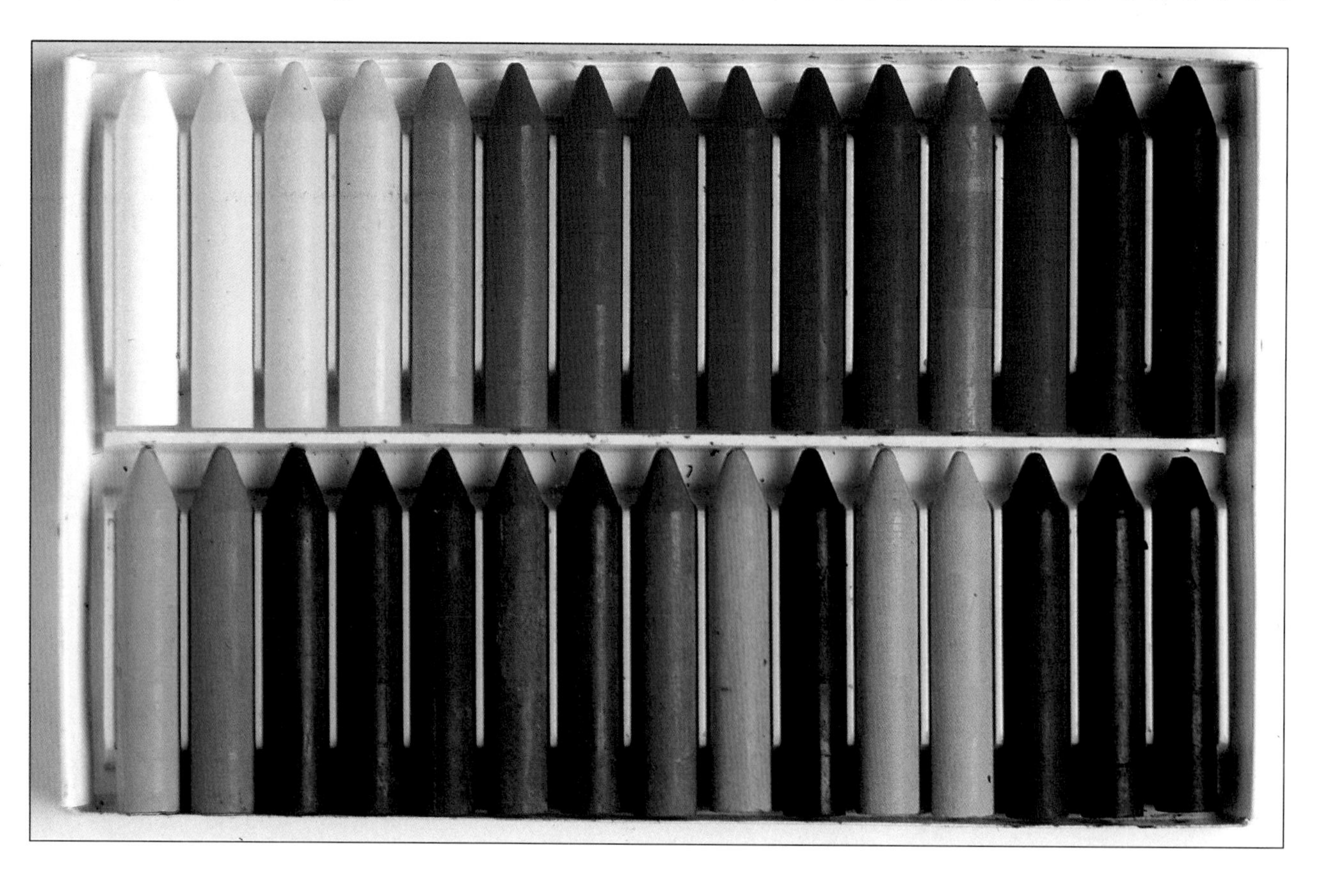

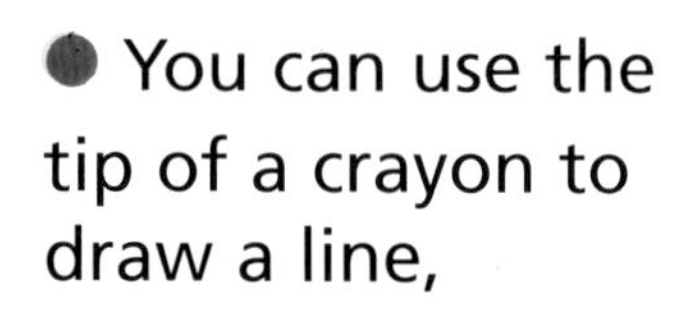

You can use the tip of a crayon to draw a line,

pressing hard,

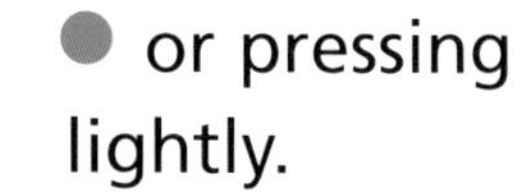

or pressing lightly.

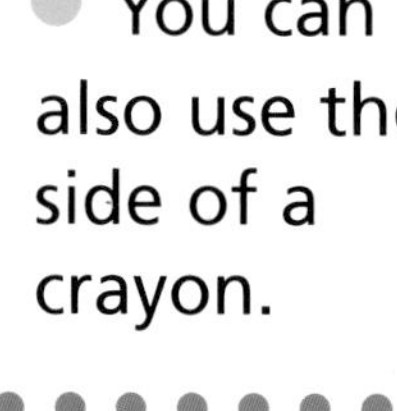

You can also use the side of a crayon.

You can also:

- use two different colors together,
- or crayon lightly so that the colors underneath show through.
- You can use the crayons on colored paper,
- smear several colors together,
- or cover one color with another.

CREATING DIFFERENT TEXTURES

When used different kinds of surfaces, wax crayons can create different textures.

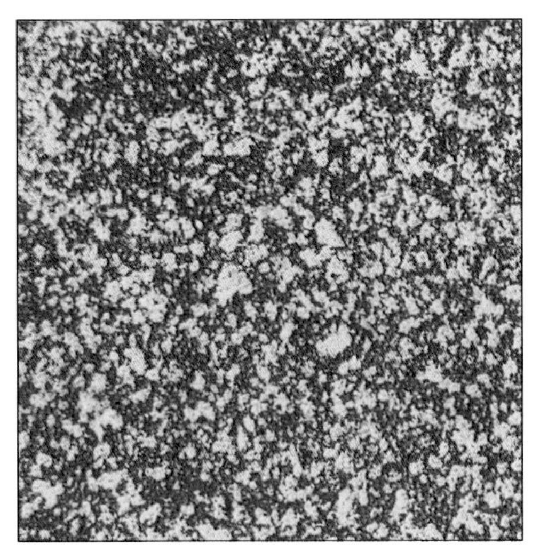

Try using crayons on a piece of sandpaper.

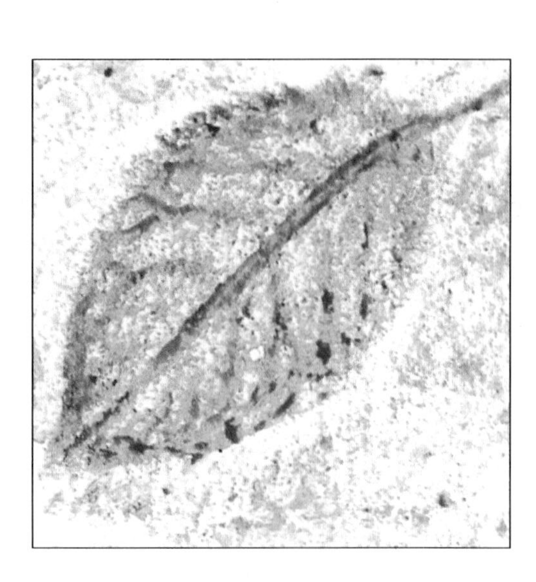

To make a leaf rubbing, place a thin piece of paper on a leaf and gently rub over the top with wax crayon.

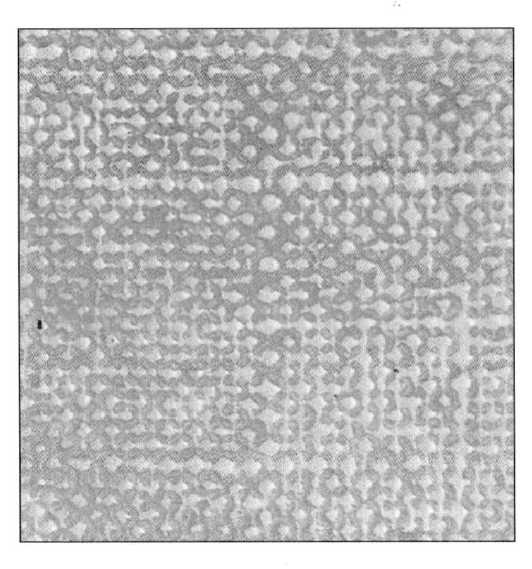

You can crayon on thick, bumpy paper

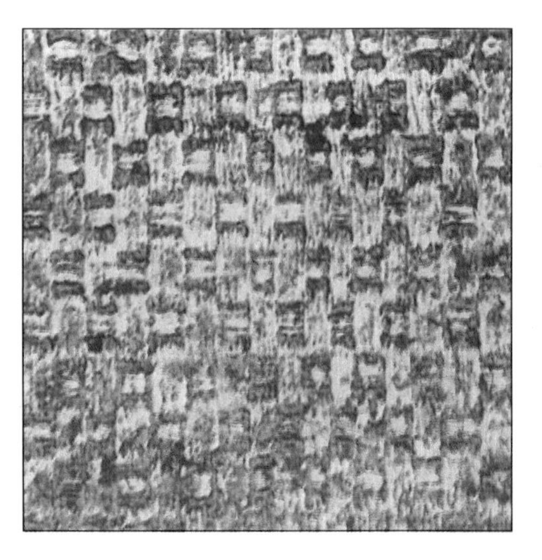

or on fabric.

Crayoning on a piece of cork can give an interesting texture.

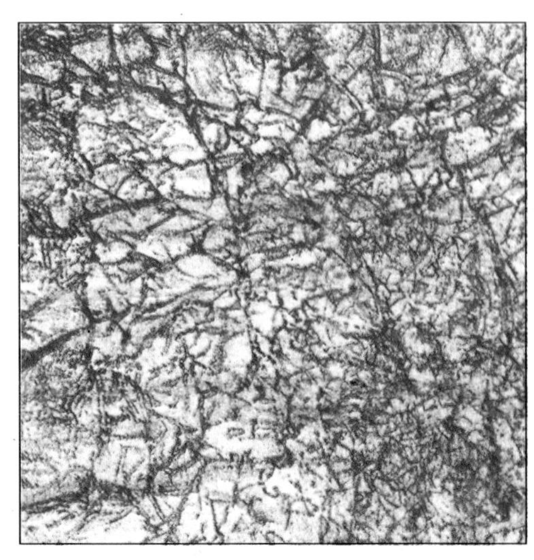

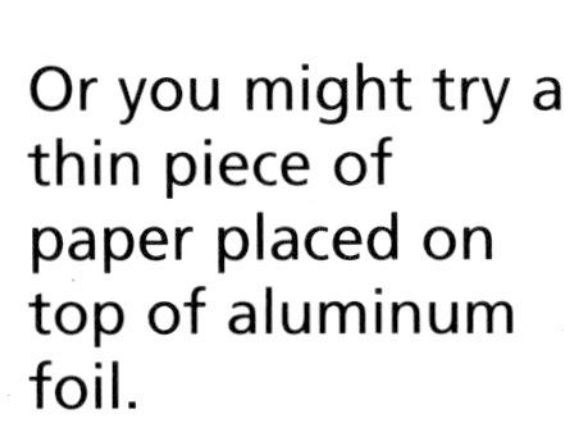

Or you might try a thin piece of paper placed on top of aluminum foil.

SCRAPING WAX CRAYONS

All kinds of different patterns can be made by scraping through a layer of wax crayon. You will need to cover a piece of paper with a thick layer of crayon. To scrape out a pattern you can use a toothpick, the cap of a pen, or the wooden end of a thin paintbrush.

Scrape out some lines.

Use two layers of different colored crayon and scrape through the top layer, to reveal the color below.

You can cover a layer of wax crayon with poster paint.

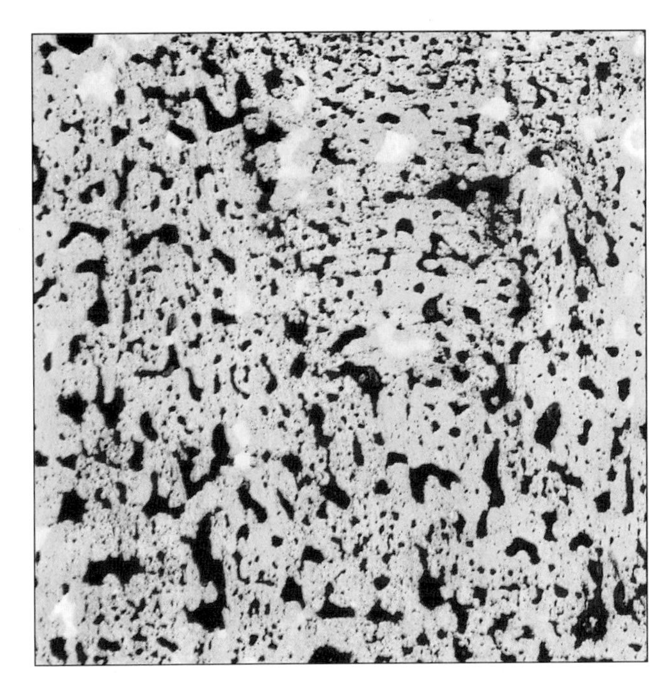

You will need to paint over the wax crayon several times, leaving the paint to dry in between each layer.

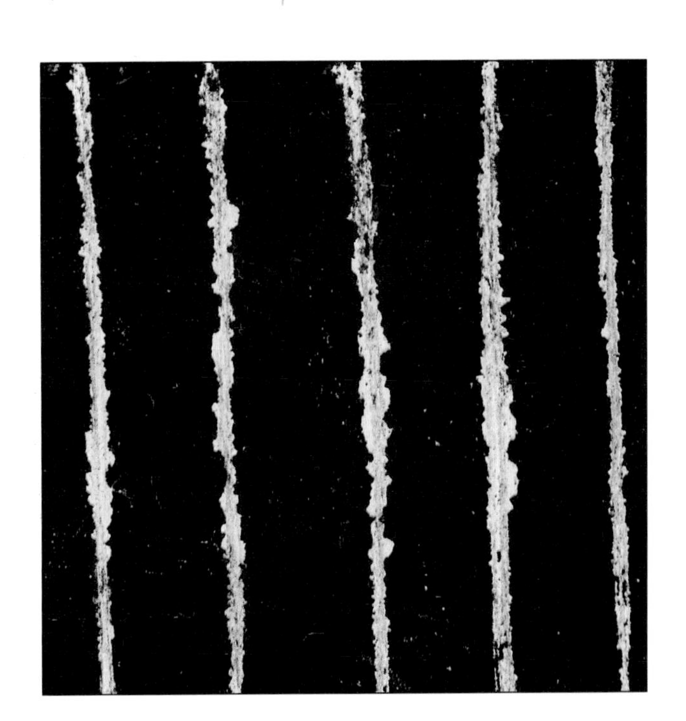

When the wax crayon is completely covered, you can scrape off some of the paint.

PAINTING OVER WAX CRAYONS

Wax crayons don't absorb paint. This makes it difficult to cover them with paint, but it can also create some interesting effects. To experiment with some of these effects, try drawing a pattern in wax crayons on four different pieces of paper. Here the artist has drawn circles and dots.

Paint over the first pattern with India ink.

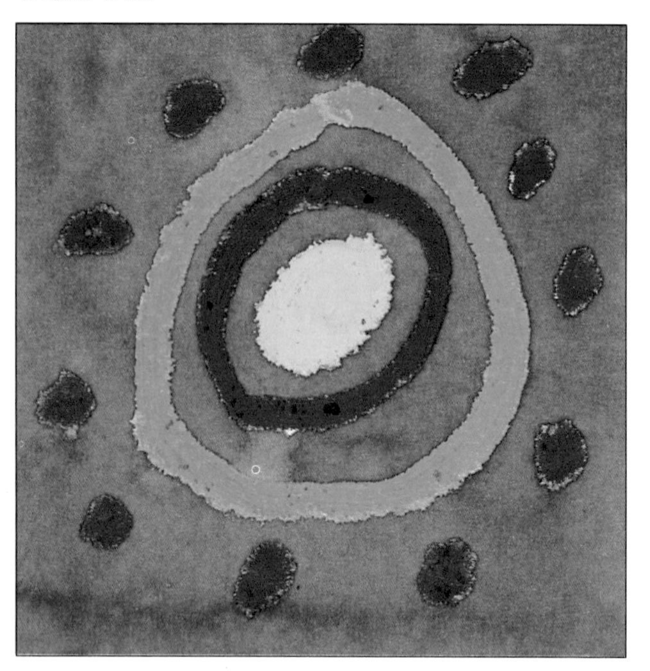

Use poster paint on the second pattern.

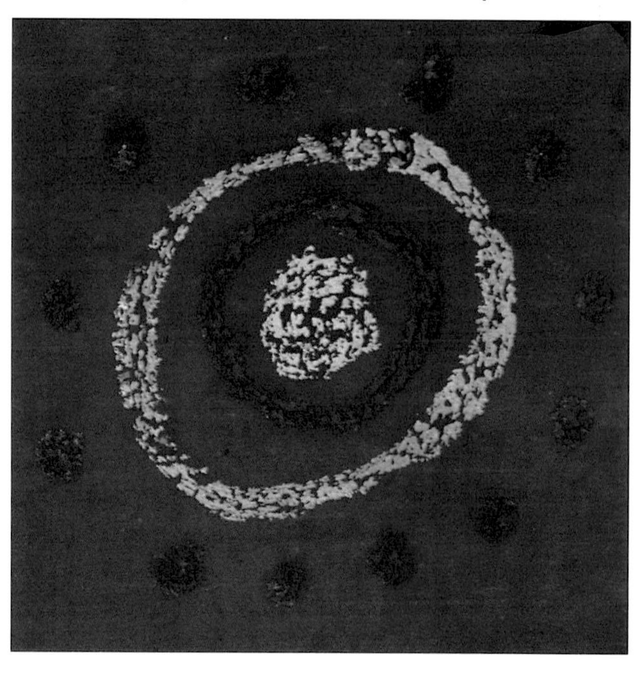

! Ask an adult to help you paint the third pattern with fabric dye.

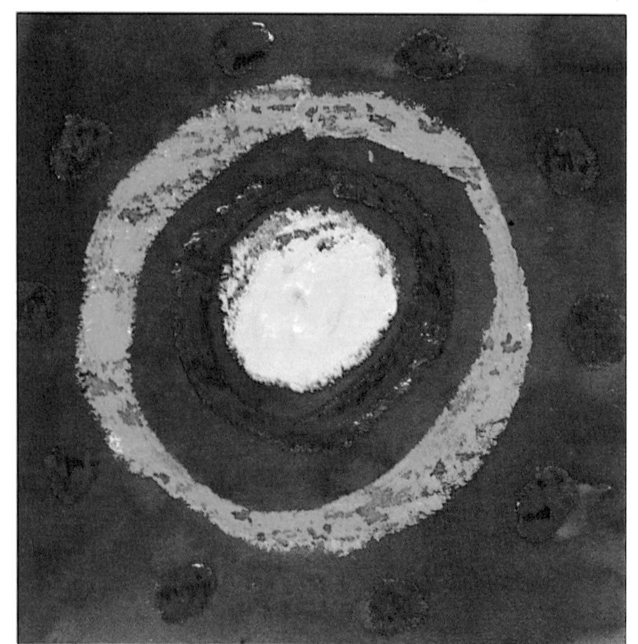

Paint over the fourth pattern with watercolors.

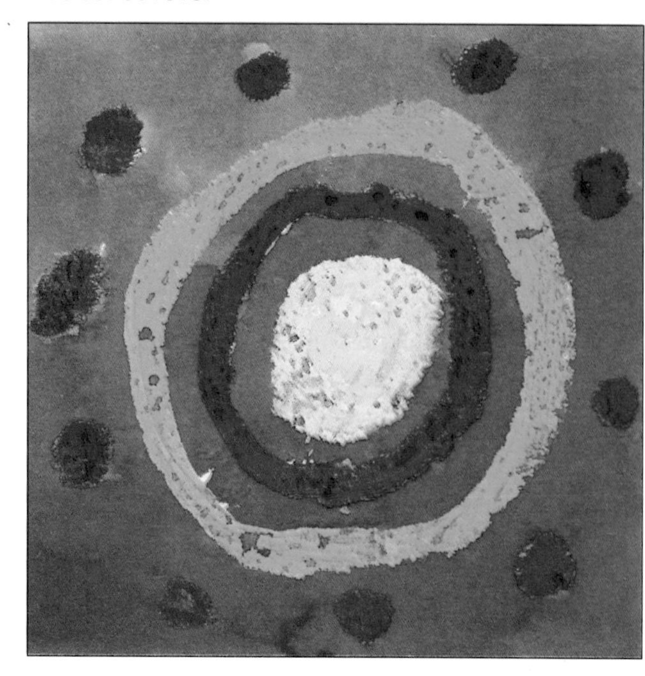

INVENT YOUR OWN TECHNIQUES

Experimenting with wax crayons and trying out your own ideas is the best way to discover new techniques. Here are some suggestions to help you get started.

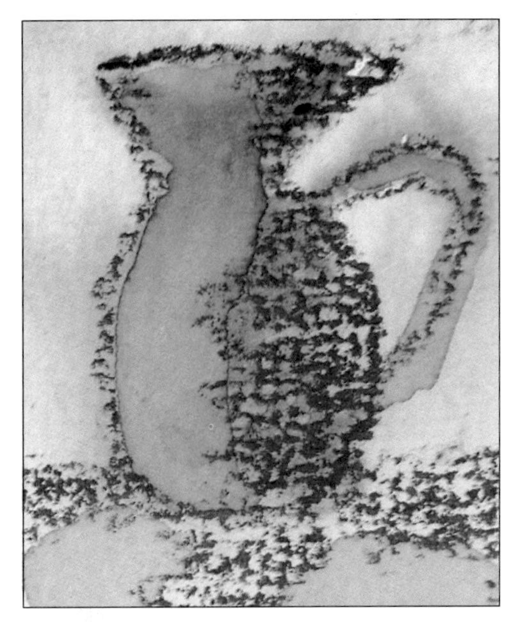

Crayon on rough paper and then paint over the top with watercolors.

Scrape a pattern out of a layer of wax crayon. Paint over the top and then scrape again.

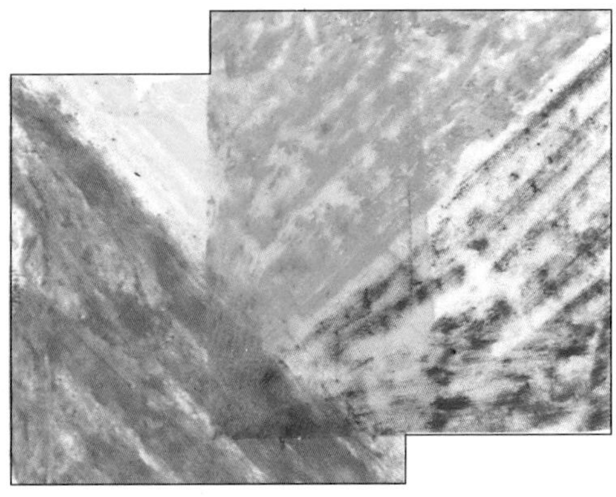

Use wax crayons to draw on a clear sheet of acetate.

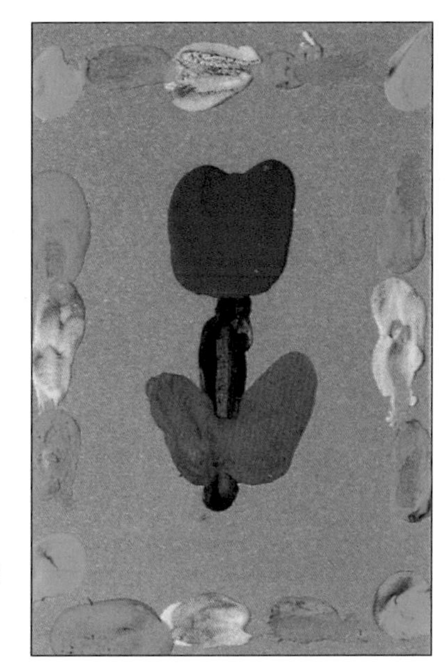

! Make a picture using small drops of melted wax crayon. You could use a candle to melt the crayon but you will need an adult to help you.

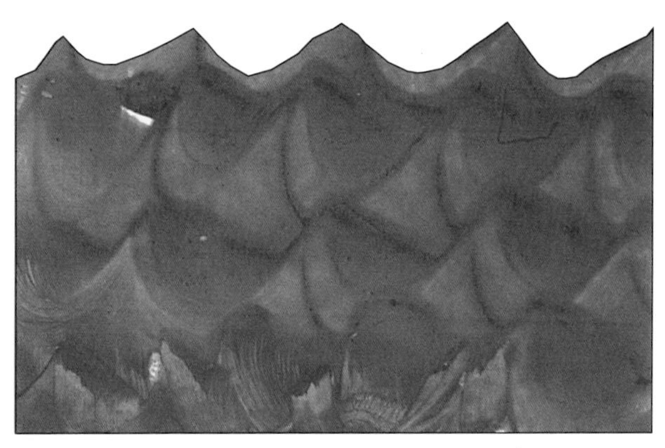

Warm your wax crayon picture by placing it in the sun or on top of a radiator.

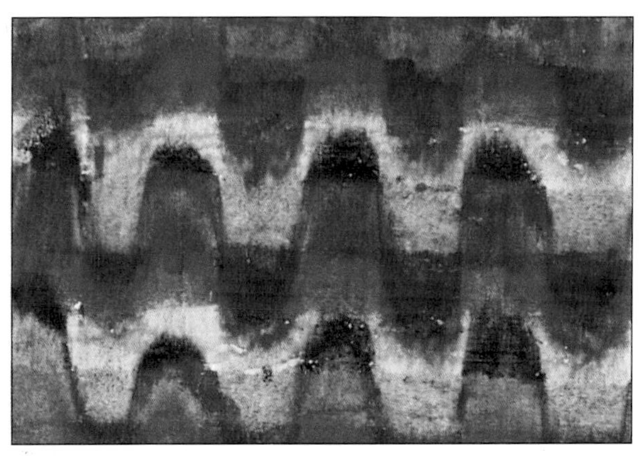

Smudge a wax crayon pattern with your finger.

TEN DIFFERENT TECHNIQUES FOR YOU TO TRY

These techniques are explained on pages 12-31 with step-by-step instructions.

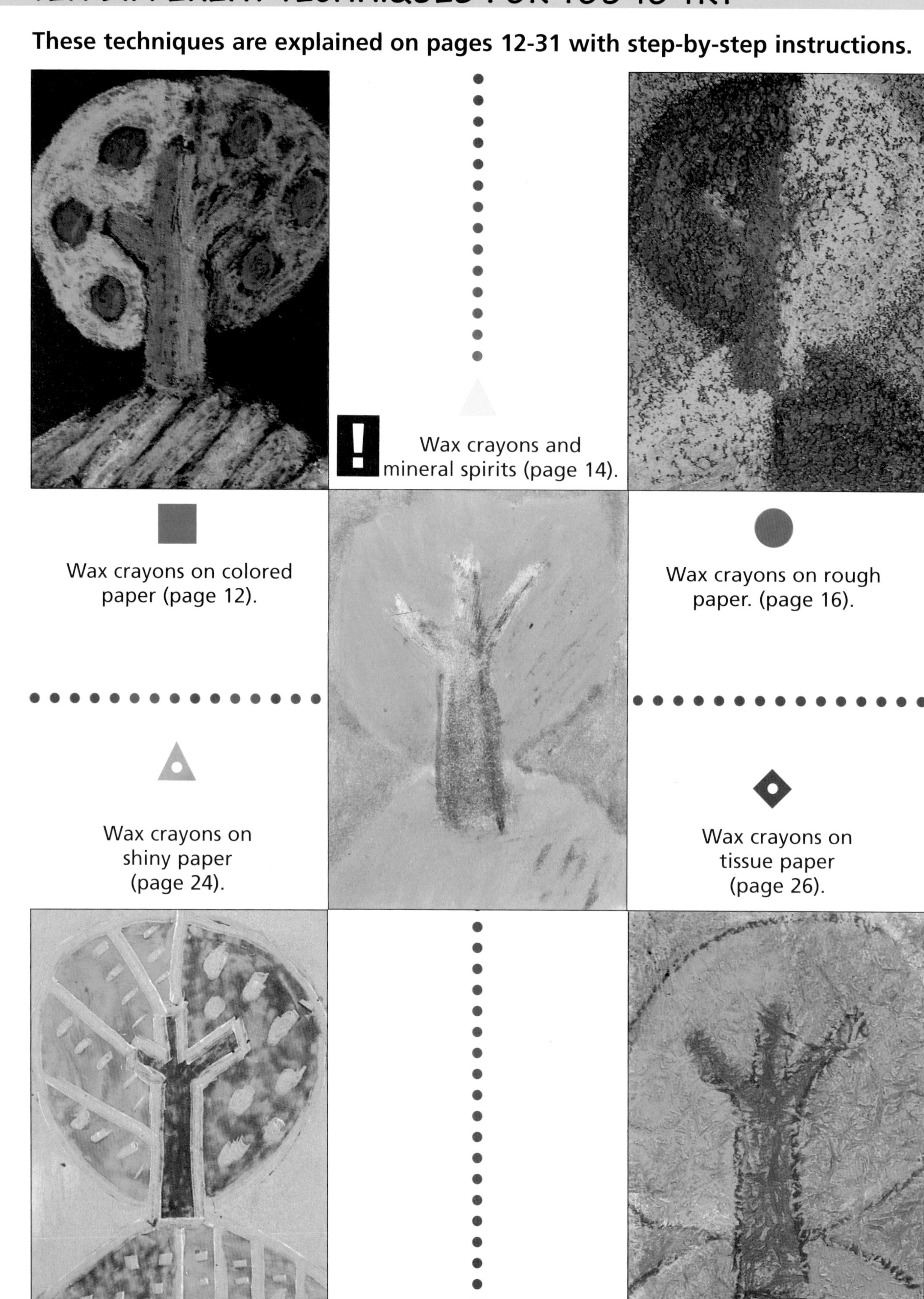

Wax crayons and mineral spirits (page 14).

Wax crayons on colored paper (page 12).

Wax crayons on rough paper. (page 16).

Wax crayons on shiny paper (page 24).

Wax crayons on tissue paper (page 26).

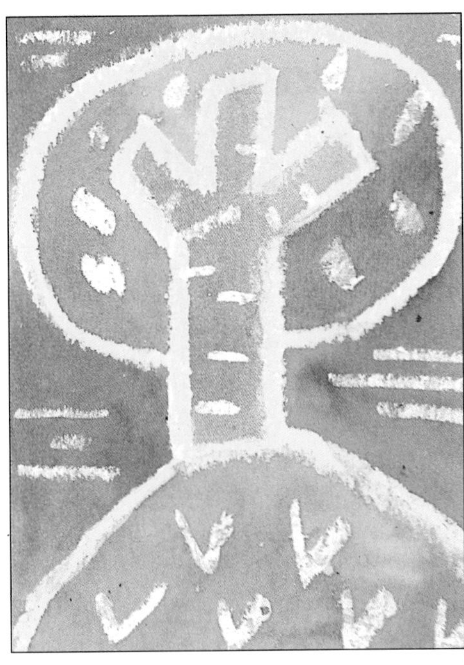

Scraped wax crayons
(page 20).

Wax crayons and
watercolors (page 18).

Wax crayons on fabric
(page 22).

!

Wax crayons and
wood stain. (page 28).

Scraped poster paint on
wax crayon (page 30).

WAX CRAYONS ON COLORED PAPER

Combining different colored wax crayons on colored paper will give very different effects. Experiment to see which colors stand out the most and which colors appear transparent.

1 On orange paper, the yellow house can hardly be seen, but the blue crayon stands out very clearly.

2 On green paper, the yellow house looks green.

3 On blue paper, the yellow house stands out more clearly.

4 White crayon on top of dark colors makes them look lighter.

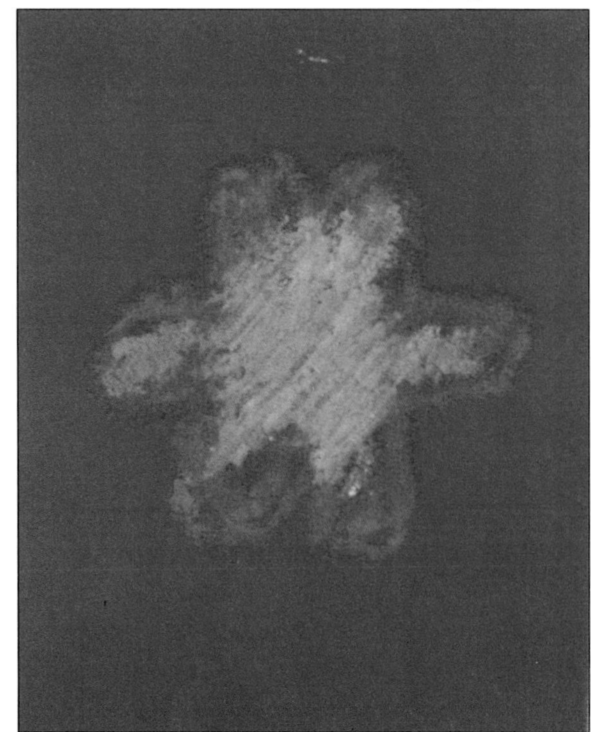

5

n black
aper, try
xperimenting
vith your
wn color
ombinations.

WAX CRAYONS AND MINERAL SPIRITS

Wax crayons can be dissolved using mineral spirits. You must ask an adult to help you.

1

Here's a green and yellow background that has been crayoned in.

2

Mineral spirits have been painted over the crayon, using brush strokes from top to bottom. Brush strokes in other directions, from left to right for example, will give a different effect.

3

This artist has added some red flowers to the picture.

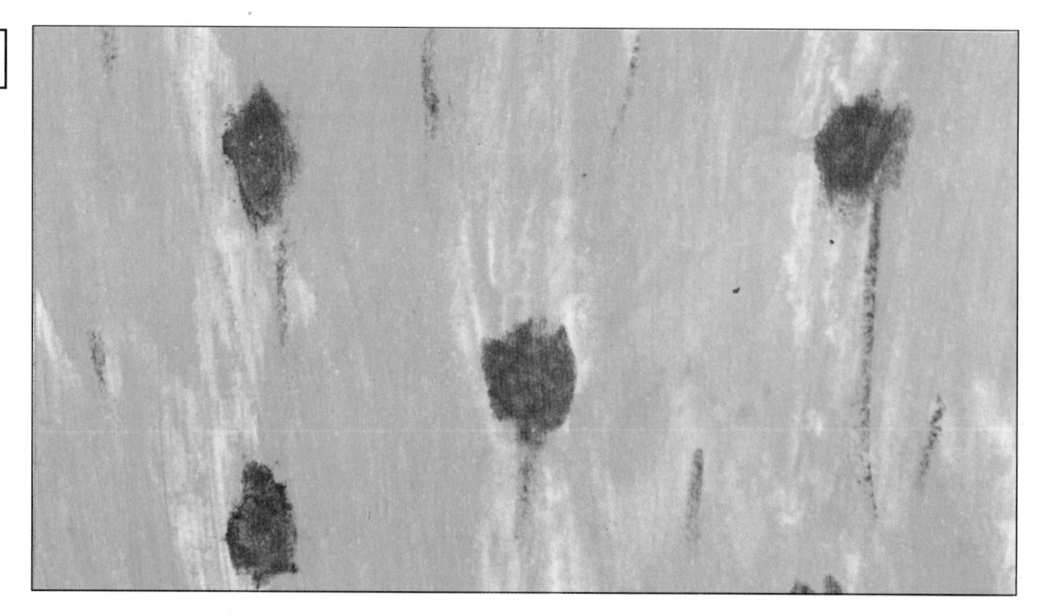

4

When the picture is dry, more objects can be added and then painted over with mineral spirits. This can be repeated until the picture is finished.

WAX CRAYONS ON ROUGH PAPER

If you use wax crayons on rough paper, the texture of the paper will show through in the picture.

1

Try crayoning an abstract design on a piece of sandpaper.

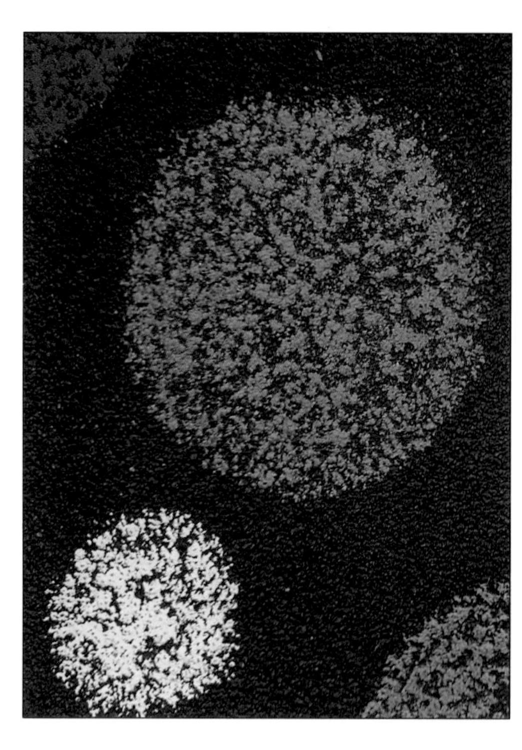

2

This artist has crayoned in a dark back-ground and colored circles.

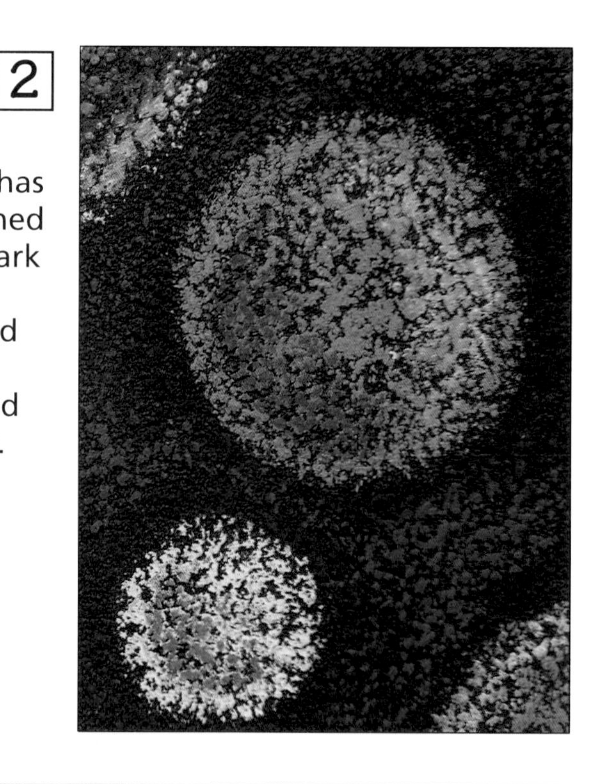

3

You can see the texture in this close-up picture.

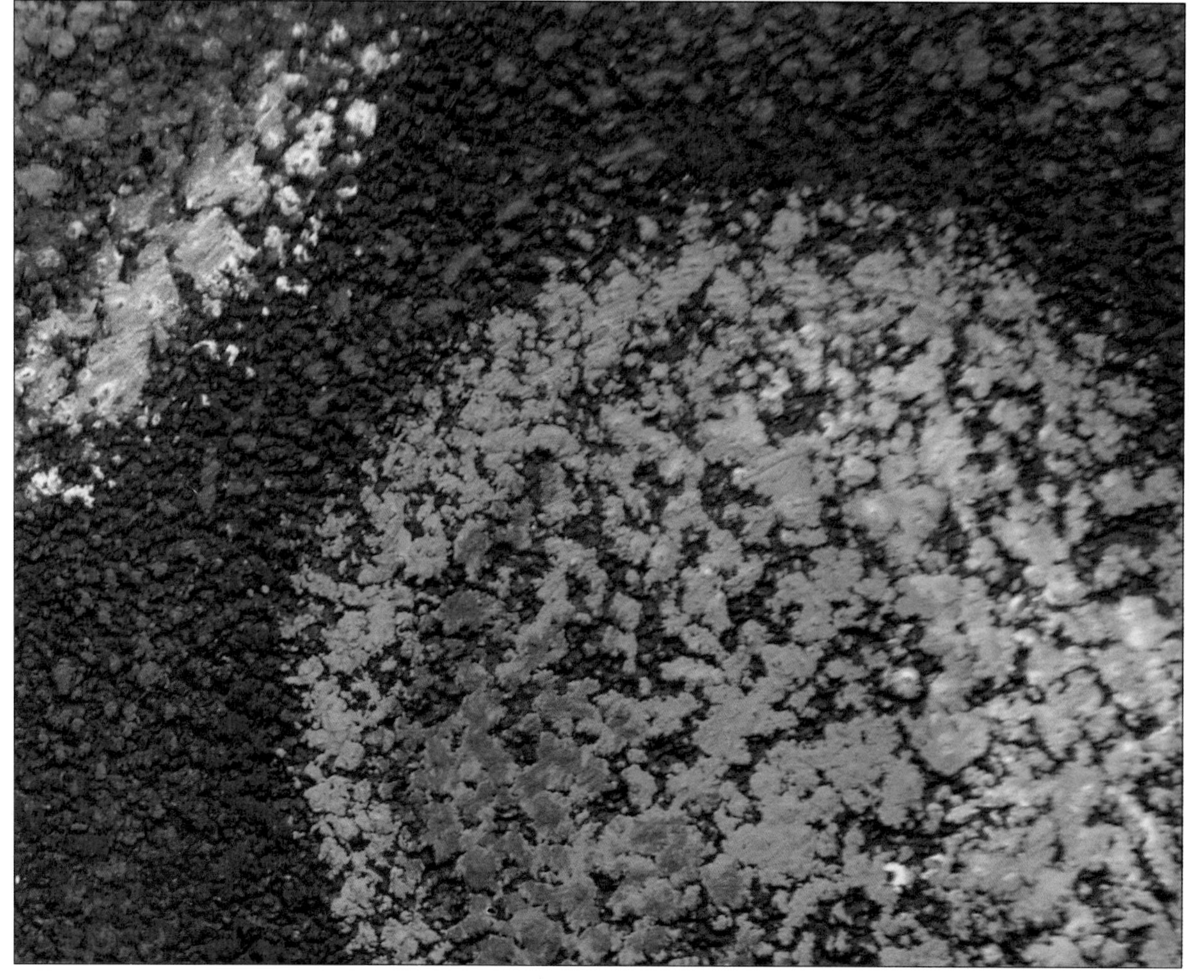

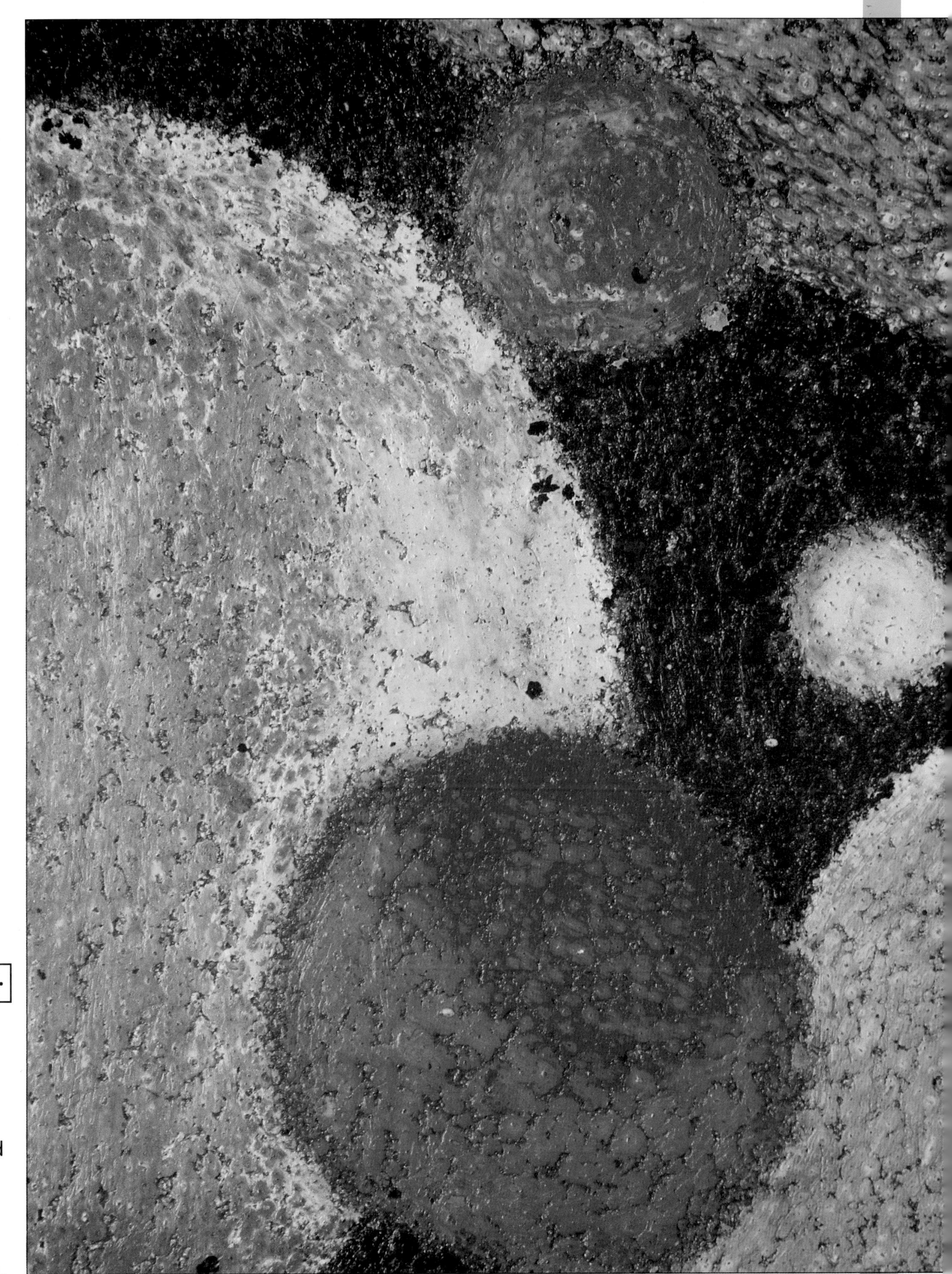

4

If you crayon some circles in different colors and sizes, you could create a space landscape.

WAX CRAYONS AND WATERCOLORS

If you paint over a wax crayon pattern with watercolors, the paint will only stay on the paper where there is no crayon.

1

This artist has drawn the leaves of a tree in wax crayon.

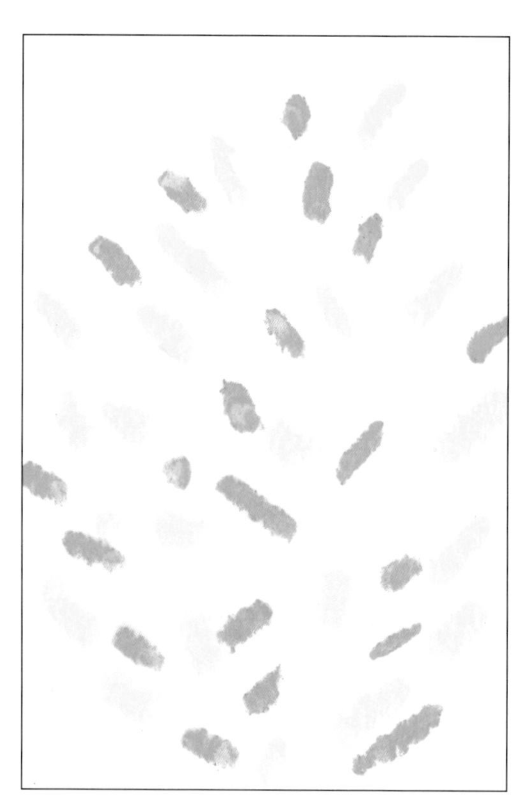

2

Then, she has painted the shape of a tree around the leaves using green water-colors. The paint won't cover the leaves.

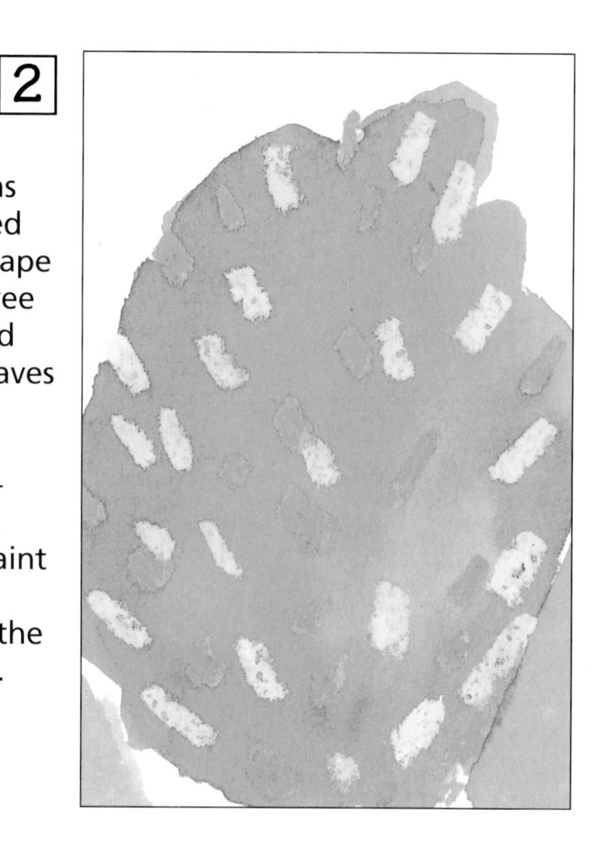

3

In this picture, the artist has used a white crayon before painting watercolors

4

You could use different colored wax crayons and watercolors to make a picture. If you don't want the watercolors to run in to each other, let each color dry before you start painting the next.

SCRAPED WAX CRAYONS

If you cover a piece of paper with two, thick layers of different colored wax crayon, you can scrape away the top layer so that the bottom layer shows through.

1

Use several bright colors to make the bottom layers.

2

With a black crayon, completely cover the bottom layer. You may need to add two or more layers of black crayon.

3

You can scrape out a picture using a toothpick, the cap of a pen, or the wooden end of a paintbrush. As you scrape, the bottom layer of crayon will show through. Some unexpected colors will appear.

4

If you make a mistake, you can crayon over the top with black crayon and start again.

This artist has created a sea, full of multicolored fish.

A piece of fabric can provide an unusual surface to draw on.

1

This artist has drawn a purple square on a piece of green cloth.

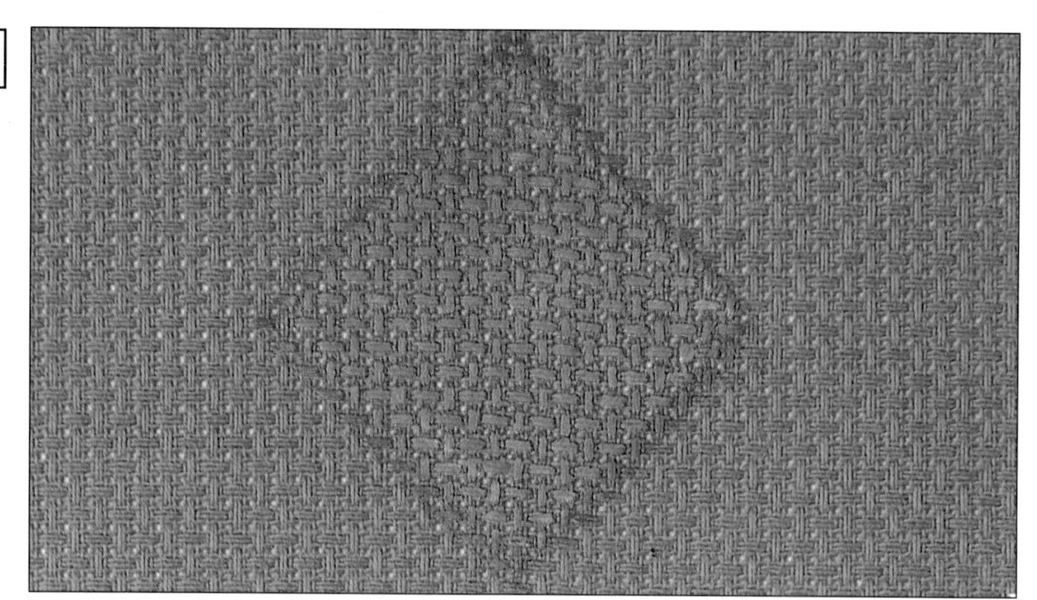

2

He then added different colored squares and triangles to build up the design.

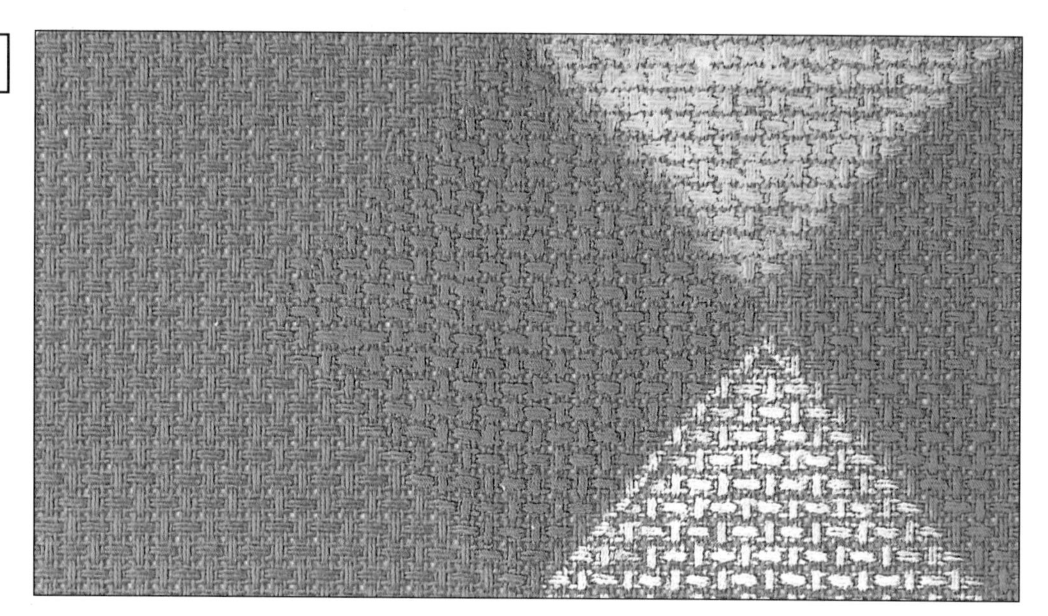

3

! To give the shapes a sharp outline, he has painted around the edges of the squares and triangles with a small paintbrush dipped in mineral spirits.

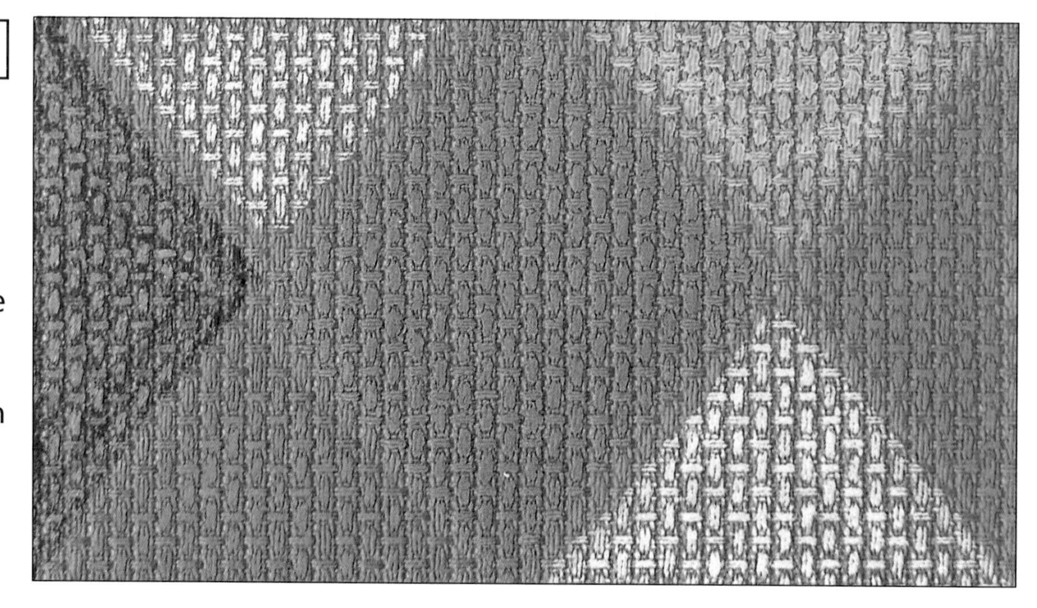

4

ry out some
atterns and
ictures on
ifferent kinds
f fabric.

WAX CRAYONS ON SHINY PAPER

A layer of wax crayon on a piece of shiny paper makes an excellent surface to scrape out different patterns.

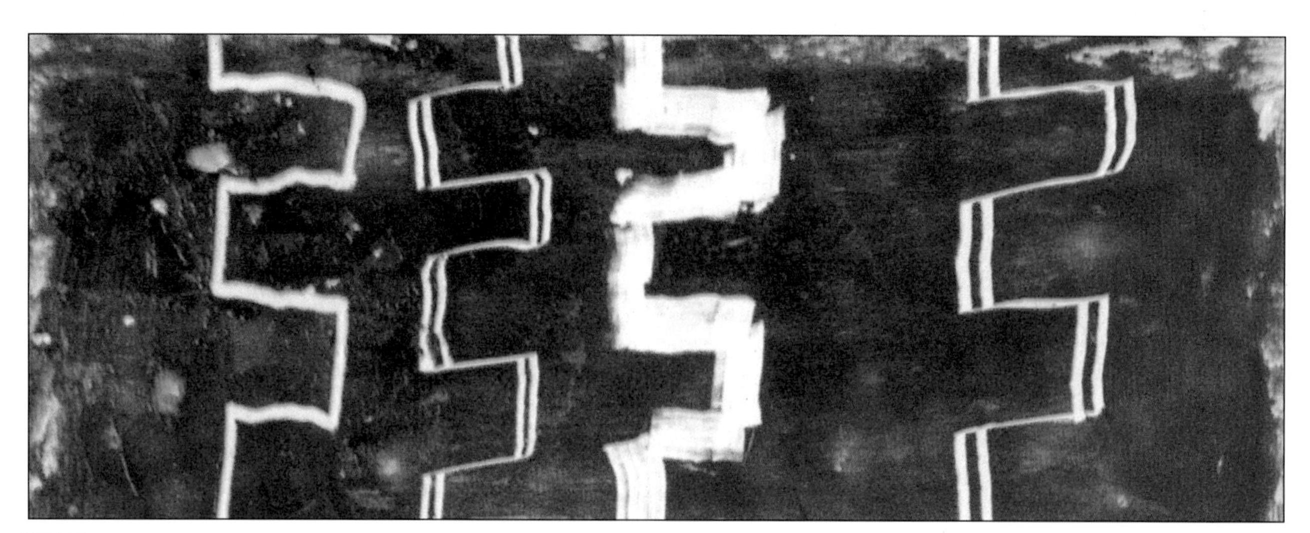

1 Cover a piece of shiny paper with a layer of wax crayon. You can experiment with different objects, such as a toothpick or a spatula, to scratch out thin and thick lines

2 This artist has crayoned a yellowed square and a blue square next to each other. She has scraped out some dots and lines.

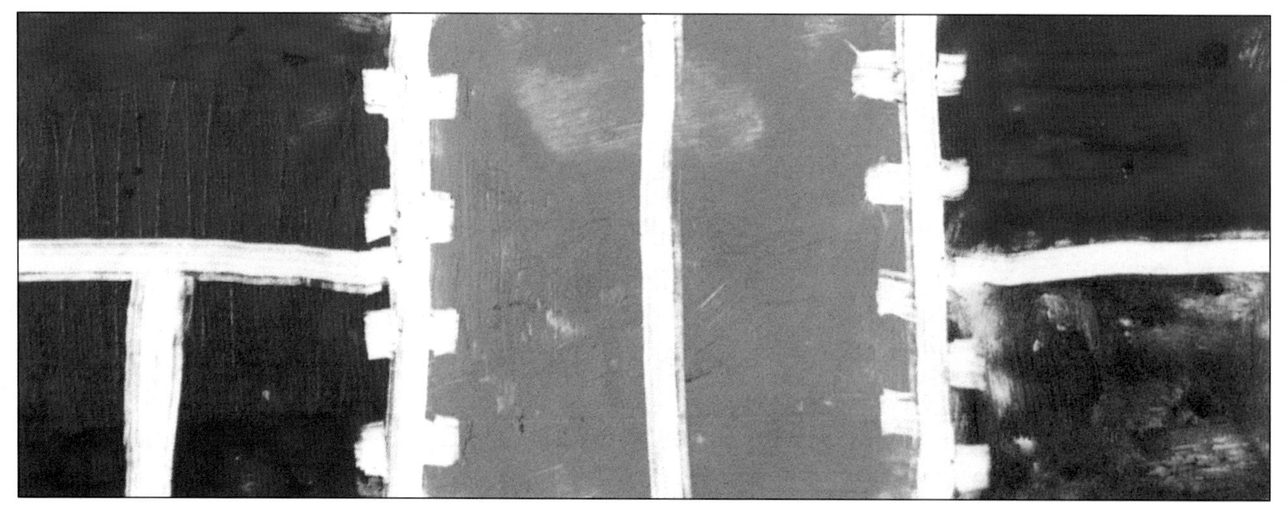

3 More colored squares can be added to build up the picture and lines can be drawn to separate the different colored squares.

4

This artist has created a town using this technique. Try out some of your own ideas.

WAX CRAYONS ON TISSUE PAPER

An unusual texture can be created if you lightly crayon over crumpled tissue pape

1. You will need a piece of posterboard for a base and several different colored sheets of tissue paper.

2. Crumple up the tissue paper and the flatten it out again. Paste one sheet creased paper onto the posterboard

3. Different shapes can be cut out of the other pieces of tissue paper and then pasted on top to build up the picture.

4. When the paper is dry, gently rub ov your picture with different colored wax crayons to make the texture of the creased tissue paper stand out.

5

This artist has used the technique to create a textured landscape.

WAX CRAYONS AND WOOD STAIN

! Some striking effects and colors can be achieved when wax crayons are painted with wood stain. You must ask an adult to help you with this.

1

Crayon in the background leaving plenty of gaps on the paper.

2

Then paint over the top using wood stain.

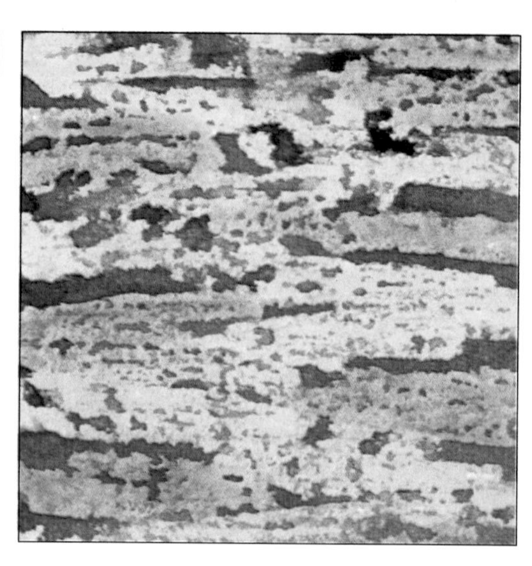

3

Steps 1 and 2 can be repeated to make more colored samples. These can be cut into different shapes.

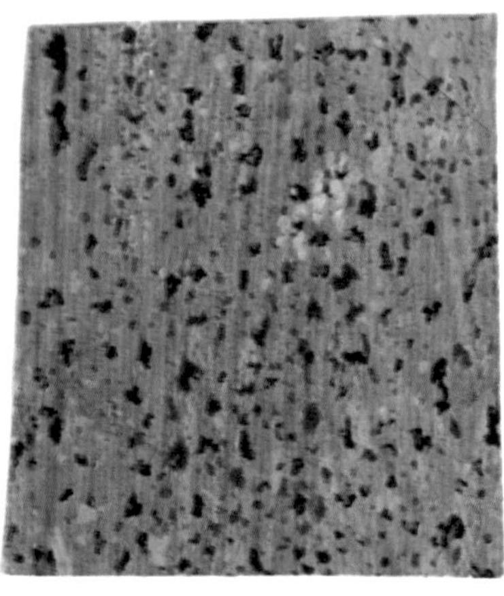

You might cut out a green forest,

a blue sky

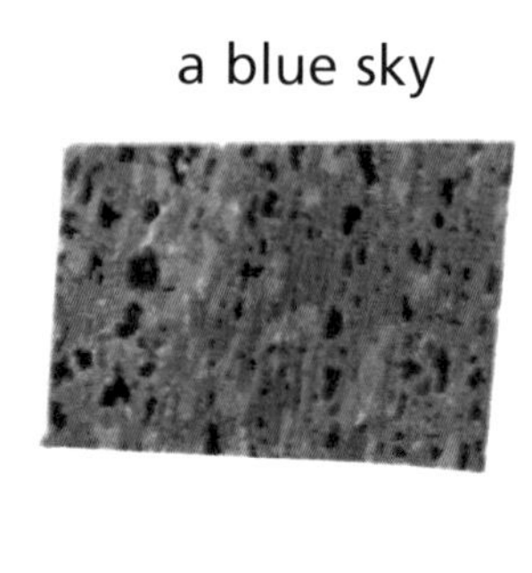

or a triangle of fire.

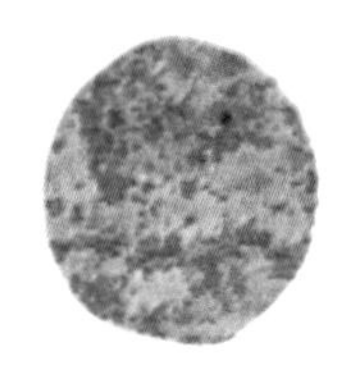

Circles could be moons,

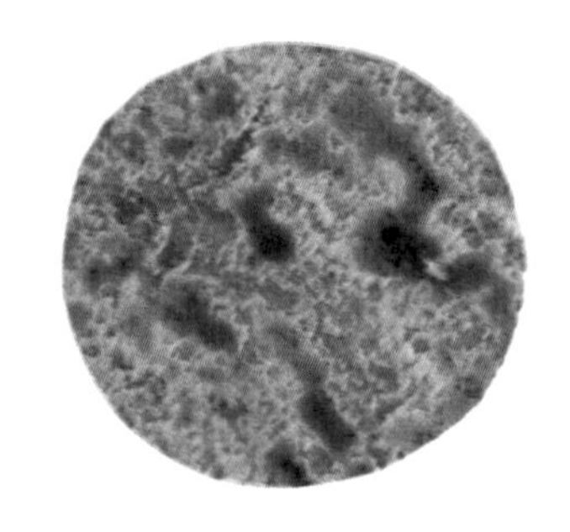

or planets.

Long curved pieces could be snakes.

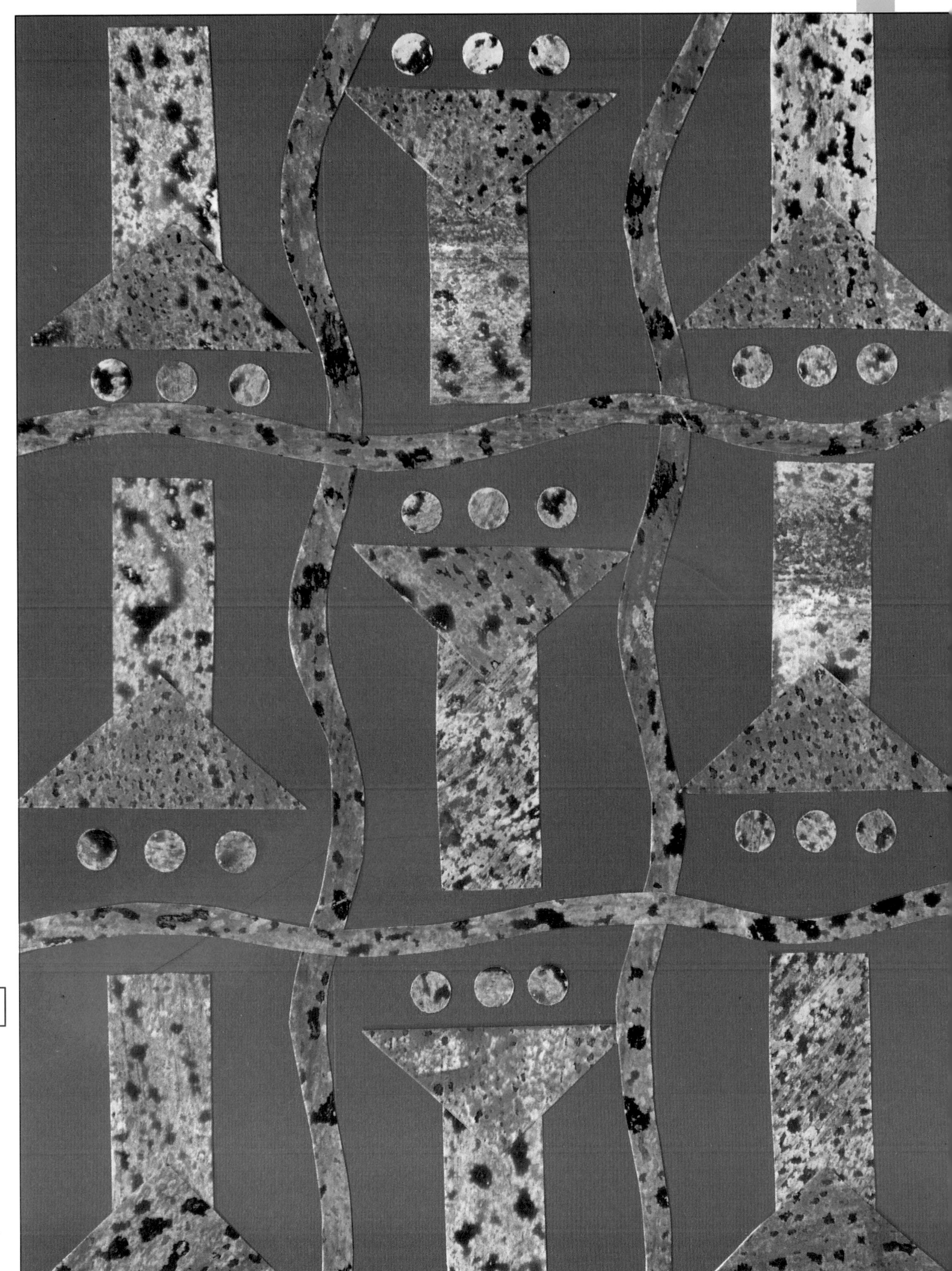

4

This artist has stuck different shapes onto a piece of red paper to make a collage.

SCRAPED POSTER PAINT ON WAX CRAYON

You can paint over a layer of wax crayon with poster paint and then scrape out a design.

1 This artist crayoned in a green and blue background.

2 Then he painted over the crayon using thick, black poster paint.

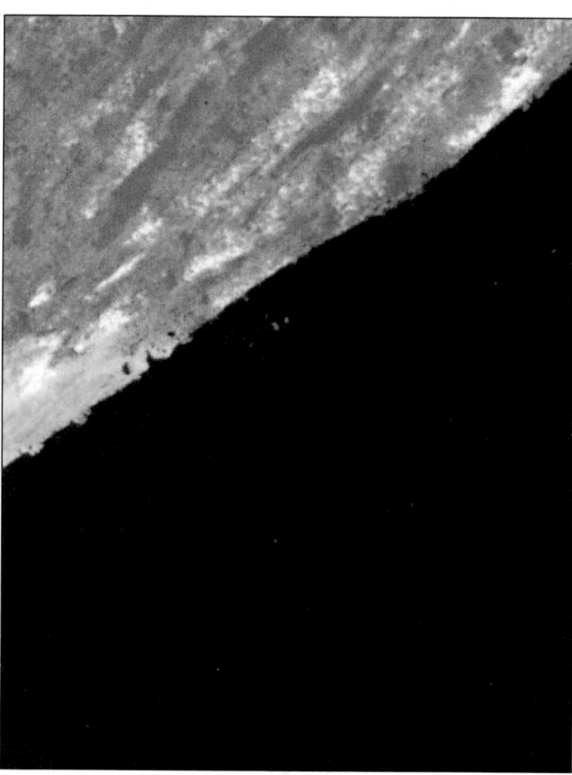

3 He scraped off the paint to leave the outline of a butterfly.

4 To make the butterfly stand out, he painted over its body with white poster paint.

5

The finished effect can make a picture look old.

INDEX

WHERE TO FIND MATERIALS

Most of the materials you will need to start working can be found in an art or stationery store. This list will give you some extra tips on where you might find materials.

Acetate This is like a piece of thick plastic which you can buy at an art store.

Cork You could use a cork tile. Ask in a hardware store. They might let you have an old tile cheaply.

Fabric Collect different kinds of fabric. Ask at home for some old clothes or old pieces of cloth.

India ink This is a special waterproof ink, which means it won't dissolve in water. You can buy it in an art supply store.

Mineral spirits This can be bought in a hardware store. You must ask an adult to buy it and help you use it.

Paper You might ask at home or in a hardware store for old pieces of paper. Try crayoning on textured wallpaper, different thicknesses of sandpaper, or greaseproof paper.

Poster paint can be bought in an art supply store or you could use ready-mixed powder paint.

Wood stain This can be bought in a hardware store. You must ask an adult to buy it and help you use it.